Bach Masterpieces
for Solo Piano
37 Works

JOHANN SEBASTIAN BACH

DOVER PUBLICATIONS, INC.
Mineola, New York

Bibliographical Note

This Dover edition, first published in 1999, is a new compilation of works originally published separately. Ferruccio Busoni's piano transcriptions were originally published by Breitkopf & Härtel, Wiesbaden, n.d. The transcription of "Jesu, Joy of Man's Desiring" was prepared specially for this edition. All other works were drawn from *Johann Sebastian Bach's Werke*, originally published by the Bach-Gesellschaft, Breitkopf & Härtel, Leipzig, 1853–94.

International Standard Book Number

ISBN-13: 978-0-486-40847-7
ISBN-10: 0-486-40847-7

Manufactured in the United States by RR Donnelley
40847705   2016
www.doverpublications.com

CONTENTS

Aria Varied in the Italian Manner

Aria variata alla maniera italiana

BWV 989 (1709)

Var. I. (Largo.)

Var. II.

Var. III.

Var. IV. (Allegro.)

Var. V. (Un poco Allegro.)

Var. VI. (Andante.)

Var. VII. (Allegro.)

Var. VIII. (Allegro.)

Capriccio on the Departure
of His Most Beloved Brother

Capriccio sopra la lontananza del suo fratello dilettissimo

BWV 992 (1704)

ARIOSO.

Adagio. Ist eine Schmeichelung der Freunde, um denselben von seiner Reise abzuhalten.

Is a wheedling by friends in order to keep him from his journey.

(Andante.) Ist eine Vorstellung unterschiedlicher Casuum, die ihm in der Fremde könnten vorfallen.

Is a setting-forth of various casualties that could befall him abroad.

Adagissimo. Ist ein allgemeines Lamento der Freunde.

Is a general *lamento* by his friends.

Allhier kommen die Freunde, weil sie doch sehen, dass es anders nicht sein kann, und nehmen Abschied.

Here the friends come, seeing after all that it cannot be otherwise, and bid farewell.

Aria di Postiglione. [Postilion's air]

Adagio poco.

Fuga all' imitazione della cornetta di postiglione. [Fugue in imitation of the postilion's horn]

Chaconne in D Minor

From *Partita II in D Minor for Violin* / BWV 1004 (1720)

Transcribed by Ferruccio Busoni (1897?)

Andante maestoso, ma non troppo lento
Feierlich gemessen, doch nicht schleppend

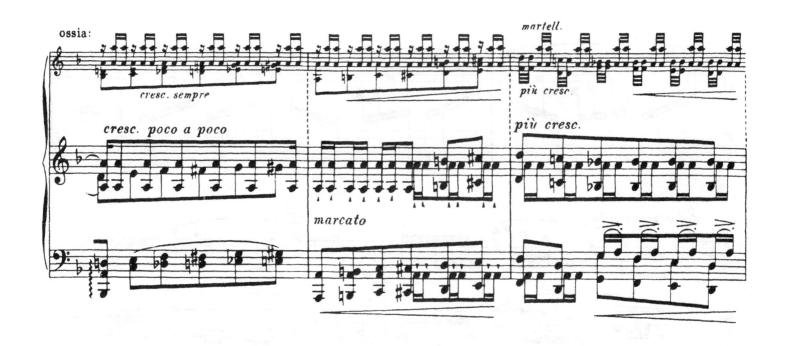

Chromatic Fantasia and Fugue in D Minor

Chromatische Fantasie und Fuge

BWV 903 (1730)

Fantasia.

Fuga.

English Suite II in A Minor

BWV 807 / From (6) *Englische Suiten* (1722)

Prélude

Allemande

Courante

Sarabande

Les agréments de la même Sarabande.

Bourrée I
(**alternativement.**)

Bourrée II

Da Capo
dal Segno 𝄋
(senza repetizione)
al Fine.

Fantasia in C Minor

BWV 906 (1738)

Fantasia and Fugue in A Minor

BWV 904 (1725)

Fantasia.

Fuga.

French Suite V in G Major

BWV 816 / From (6) *Französische Suiten* (1722)

Allemande

Courante

Sarabande

Gavotte

Bourrée I

Bourrée II

Gigue

Goldberg Variations

Three excerpts from *Aria mit 30 Veränderungen* / BWV 988 (1742)
"Goldberg Variationen" from *Klavierübung*, Part IV

Aria

Variatio 25

Variatio 30: Quodlibet

Aria da Capo e Fine.

Invention 1 in C Major

BWV 772 / From 15 two-part *Inventionen* (1720–23)

Invention 8 in F Major

BWV 779 / From 15 two-part *Inventionen* (1720–23)

Invention 9 in F Minor

BWV 780 / From 15 two-part *Inventionen* (1720–23)

Invention 10 in G Major

BWV 781 / From 15 two-part *Inventionen* (1720–23)

Invention 14 in B-flat Major

BWV 785 / From 15 two-part *Inventionen* (1720–23)

Sinfonia 9 in F Minor

BWV 795 / From 15 three-part *Sinfonien* (1720–23)

Sinfonia 15 in B Minor

BWV 801 / From 15 three-part *Sinfonien* (1720–23)

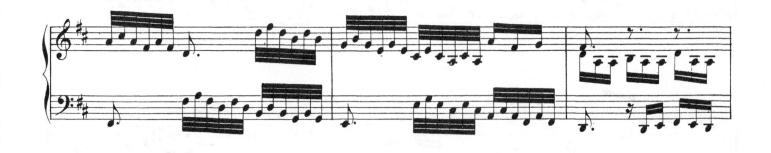

"Jesu, Joy of Man's Desiring"

Chorale from Cantata 147, "Herz und Mund und Tat und Leben" (1717)

Keyboard reduction from the full score by Ronald Herder

Italian Concerto

Italienisches Konzert

BWV 971 (1734) / From *Klavierübung*, Part IV

I. [Allegro]

II. Andante

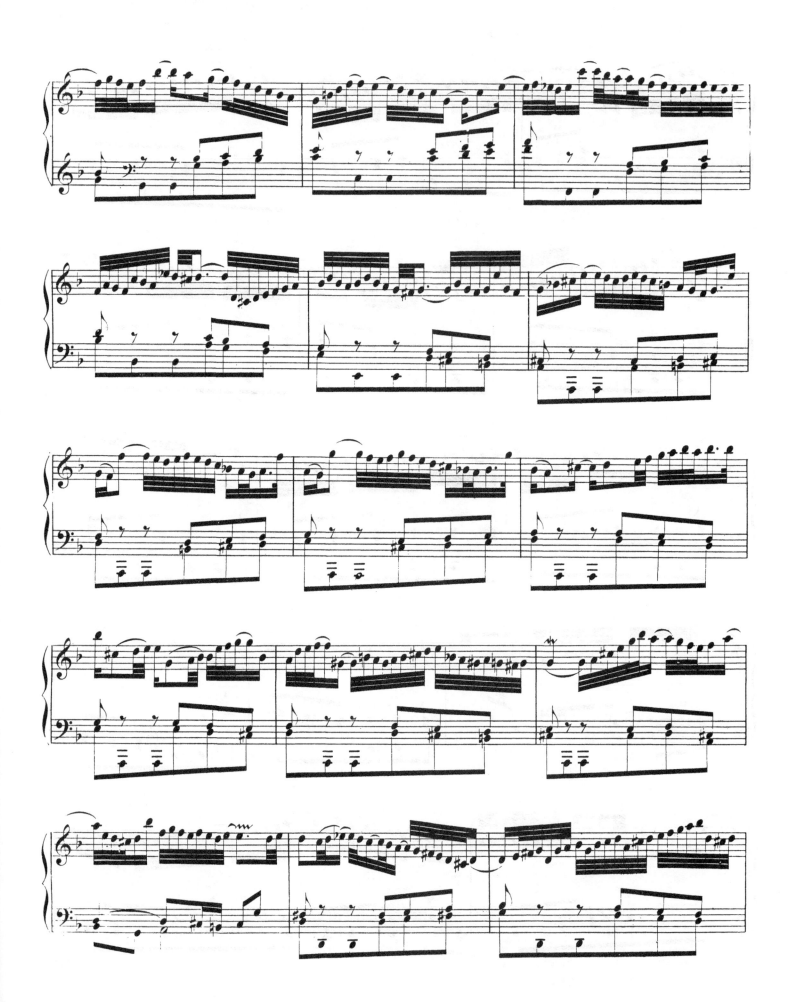

III. Presto

forte

Three Minuets

BWV 841–3 / From *Klavierbüchlein für Wilhelm Friedemann Bach* (1720–21)

Seven Little Preludes

BWV 924–930 / From *Klavierbüchlein für Wilhelm Friedemann Bach* (1720–21)

1.

"Sleepers, Awake"

Organ chorale-prelude, BWV 645

Based on Cantata 140, "Wachet auf, ruft uns die Stimme" (1731?)

Transcribed for piano by Ferruccio Busoni (ca. 1907)

Allegretto tranquillo

Mit dem einfachen Ausdruck naiver Frömmigkeit
Con semplicità devota
mezza voce, egualmente

Pedalgebrauch sehr diskret
Si usi del pedale con molta riservatezza

Der Baß etwas mit Bedeutung
Il basso con un poco di rilievo

Overture in the French Style

[Partita in B Minor]

BWV 831 (1734) / From *Klavierübung*, Part II

Ouverture

Courante

Gavotte I

Gavotte II

Passepied II

Passepied I Da Capo.

Sarabande

Bourrée I

Bourrée II

Gigue

Echo

Prelude and Fugue No. 1 in C Major

BWV 846 / From *Das Wohltemperierte Klavier*, Book I (1722)

Prelude and Fugue No. 2 in C Minor

BWV 847 / From *Das Wohltemperierte Klavier*, Book I (1722)

Allegro ♩ = 108 (Tovey: slower)

Prelude and Fugue No. 5 in D Major

BWV 850 / From *Das Wohltemperierte Klavier*, Book I (1722)

Vivace ♩ = 132 (Tovey: *a shade slower*)

Allegro moderato ♩ = 80
(Tovey: slower; in French overture style)
a 4.

Prelude and Fugue No. 12 in F Minor

BWV 881 / From *Das Wohltemperierte Klavier*, Book II (1744)

Allegretto ♩ = 88 (Tovey: faster; vivace)

Partita I in B-flat Major

BWV 825 (1726) / From *Klavierübung*, Part I

Praeludium

Allemande

Courante

Sarabande

Menuet I

Menuet II

Gigue

Toccata in C Minor

BWV 911 (1720)

Adagio.

Toccata and Fugue in D Minor

BWV 565 (1709)

Transcribed by Ferruccio Busoni (1900) from the original for organ

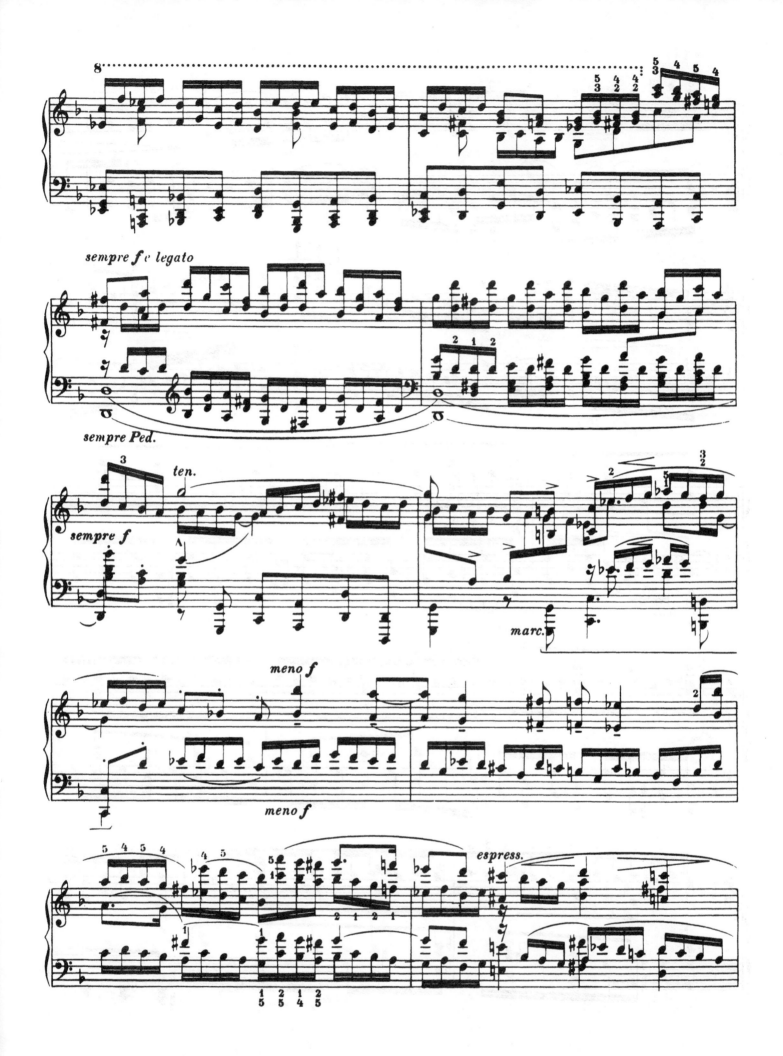

END OF EDITION